The Desires of A Woman

LAVELLE PUBLISHING

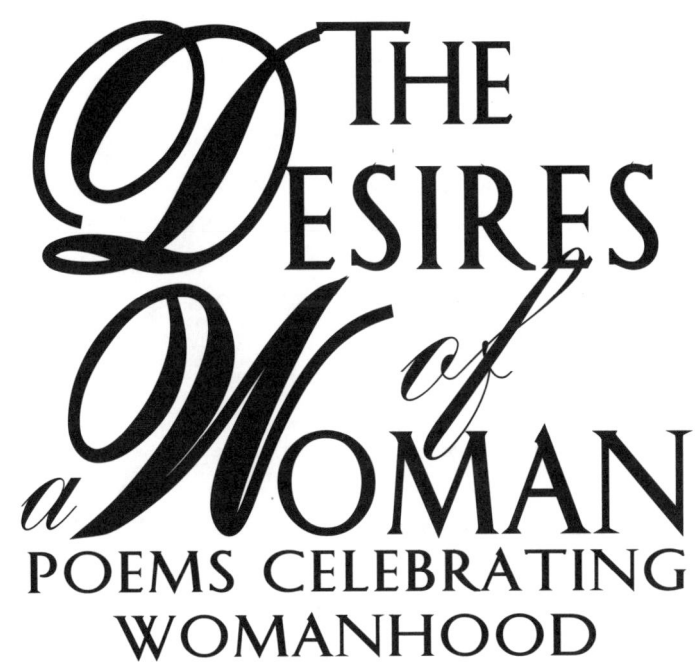

The Desires of a Woman
Poems Celebrating Womanhood

Tajuana Butler

The Desires of A Woman
Copyright © 1997 by Tajuana Butler
Published by Lavelle Publishing

Second Printing

All rights reserved. Printed in the United States of America. No part of this book may be used or reproduced in any manner whatsoever or by any means, electronic or mechanical, including photocopying, recording or by any information storage and retrieval system without written permission from the poet except in the case of brief quotations embodied in critical articles and reviews.

Manufactured in the United States of America

Front Cover Illustration by Marlon Woods
Cover designed by:
CORDELE ARTS, INC., ATLANTA

Dedication

*I dedicate this book
to my sisters, Kim and Tracy,
my mother, Linda
and my beautiful niece, Jalyn,
may life bring you the
desires of your hearts.*

*And to my daddy, Raymond.
Even when I'm 50, I'll still be
daddy's little girl.*

Acknowledgements

I am grateful for the love and support I have received while attempting to achieve my dreams. I could not ask God for a better set of family and friends.

To momma and daddy, thanks for believing in my decision to take the road less traveled.

To my sisters, thanks for appreciating and loving me unconditionally.

To Caren, my best friend, you are truly my inspiration. If I possessed half your drive, I would be unstoppable. Thanks for being my editor.

To my sands, Angie, Kim, Elisa, Crystal, Monique and Melissa, who bring new meaning to real sisterhood.

To all of my beautiful aunts, thanks for being mirrors, reflecting images of true womanhood.

Contents

Preface ix

The Desires of A Woman 1

Romance
Feeling This Feeling 9
My Fantasy 11
Earthquake 13
His Touch 17
Whisper... 19

Self Respect
Celebrating Me 23
ME 25
We Sisters 29
My Bath 33

Spiritual Growth
A Prayer For My Sisters 37
Balancing Act 41
Dear Doubt 47
A Prayer For Wisdom 49

PREFACE

Within each of us lies a need to feel complete. Although I do not believe it is possible to achieve ongoing total satisfaction, I am convinced of the possibility of experiencing moments of complete fulfillment. To become more acquainted with these moments, it is necessary to know what we need in our lives to move from desiring to realizing. We must find the courage to acknowledge that settling for a situation because of fear or lack of confidence will keep us from growing and truly attaining our desires. Although I don't have all the answers, I do know from personal experience that committing to spiritual growth can open the door to achieving self respect and fulfilling the desires we hold dear to our hearts.

You have been promised life and life more abundantly. If you believe and persevere, through inevitable adversity, you can have all the things that you want out of life. So while you continue through this book I ask that you think about your life. What are your desires, your dreams, your goals? What are the things that you want to accomplish? What are the things that you need to feel more complete, more whole? My hope is that you will be inspired to take action concerning your life and feel moved to reach to new heights of excellence, spirituality, and awareness of your womanhood. And in the process, I hope that you will be entertained.

Enjoy!

The Desires of A Woman

the desires of a WOMAN

Since you inquired I will confess
and give your mind a much needed rest.
The desires of a woman are not so complex.

The simple things we request
are things that somewhere deep all men possess.
It's the itty-bity possessions you wouldn't suspect.

You can search the world from coast to coast,
but if you think too hard and don't listen close
you still won't know the things women crave the most.

You are mistaken it's not fortune and fame,
and we sure don't have time for immature games.
That which we wish has nothing to do with pain.

We are as delicate as precious flowers that bloom.
But men, if you don't change relationships are doomed.
So listen close, for there's no time to presume.

A woman desires but to be loved,
not to be taken for granted, misused or snubbed.
It's just that simple, a woman needs love.

And not the kind that has stipulations.
A woman can do without manipulation.

What we'd prefer is communication.

Respecting our womanhood in every situation,
along with a touch of honesty and consideration.
Those are the things that bring us stimulation.

When the desires of a woman are met
her passion grows, she is at her best
and the love she shares, you'll never forget.

Since a woman makes a man complete,
we want our men to give us what we need;
Quench our desires and realize we are queens.

A Woman Desires...

...Romance

feeling this FEELING

Just when I thought it couldn't happen again.
I was beyond falling for another man, but you got me feeling this feeling again.

I thought I wouldn't get in so deep, but now you got me losing sleep.
Baby, you got me feeling this feeling again.

My mind was set.
Any amount of money I would have bet
that you couldn't make me feel this feeling again.

But you took your time.
Now your lovin' is in my soul, on my mind,
and I can't stop feeling this feeling again.

So if you will stay with me for a while
and keep flashing that handsome smile,
I'll never stop feeling this feeling again.

my FANTASY

I dream about a man who's gentle and kind
and it doesn't hurt when the brother is fine.
With a charming smile and a personality to match,
this kind of man would be a perfect catch.

You know the kind who's intelligent, yet rugged
and always finds time for kissing and hugging.
Taking the time to please and know me
are the things he'd do to make me happy.

I love a man who takes his time
and pours romance like a bottle of fine wine.
Who knows what to do to quench my desires.
I'd be on this man like a moth to the fire.

Oh, his touch and caress, they'd drive me wild.
A sensual man, yeah that's my style.
A man who knows just enough
to keep me coming back for his sweet, sweet touch.

To find the man to fit this mold
I'd pay rubies, diamonds, silver and gold.
To be with this man for just one day would make my life well worth the wait.

*earth*QUAKE

It was at a night club that I first saw him...
    ...well to be honest, the earth didn't move.

But then we danced and I looked at him and of course he was checking me out...
    ...but to be honest, the earth still didn't move.
Then we sat down at the bar and had a few drinks and talked.

You know, the usual...
He asked
    "Can I call you?"
    "When can I see you again?"

And commented
    "Aaaahhh, you look nice tonight."
(Well, I already knew that!)

There was no magic...
    ...That is until
that slow song started dragging
and he gently took my hand and led
me to the dance floor.

He pulled me so close to him.

I DON'T REMEMBER THERE BEING AN EARTHQUAKE IN THE FORECAST!

I can't think straight
Does anybody else feel the EARTH MOVING?
I can't believe this...
    ...I...I think I'm in love!

The music is softly playing...
    ...but the EARTH IS MOVING 1,000 MILES PER HOUR.
Our bodies move in slow motion...
    ...but the EARTH IS SHAKING OUT OF CONTROL
Everybody in the place is calm...
    ...but the EARTHQUAKE moves through my soul!

his TOUCH

Don't get me wrong
I am sophisticated and strong,
but nothing makes me weak
like the touch of a black man!

Now, I'm usually composed
and can stand on my own,
but nothing blows my mind
like the touch of a black man.

I'm self-assured and self-sufficient
and you better believe I'm independent,
but nothing makes me appreciate
dependence
like the touch of a black man.

I don't think you hear me. Though
I'm a lady where ever I go:
I lose my cool. I break my own rules
when I feel the touch of a black man.

whisper...

Whisper in my ear soothing words.
Words that move
through me like the ocean waves,
in the cool warm breeze,
flowing towards the sands of the beach.

Hold me in your strong embrace.
An embrace that protects me
from drowning,
That holds me above
the depth of the tide.

Kiss my lips with your wet love.
The kind of love that floats
into my heart,
And lulls me into a deep ecstasy
of overflowing emotion.

Melt my heart with your passion.
A passion that swims me safely
to the shore,
That floods my life
with joy.

...Self **Respect**

celebrating ME

I'm going all out.
I'm gonna dance, sing and shout!
'Cause in my mind there is no doubt
that today is all about
Celebrating Me!

I'm making it a big deal.
I'm partying from dawn until...
I have to express how I feel.
And you better believe it's real,
I'm Celebrating Me!

For all the situations I've come
through.
Trials and tribulations, I've had more
than a few.

But I am triumphant, I am made anew,
and as refreshed as the morning dew.
I'm Celebrating Me!

Although at times I stumble and fall
today I'm standing proud and tall.
And you ought to know I'm having a ball,
cause victory is my motto, it's my call
in Celebration of a conqueror, Me.

And when it's time for me to sleep
this joy I will still hold deep.
It's a feeling I will always keep,
in remembrance of the day I was able to reap
and Celebrate Me!

ME

I look in the mirror and I ask myself,
"What does it mean to be me?"

I stare at me.

The answer appears
> in my eyes
> on my face
> in my hands
> by the curve of my shape.

These eyes tell a story of
pain and joy, love and hate.
They know what it means to live
and they know their fate.

On my face are rivers that worry
and oceans that wave fierce.
My skin trembles and it sags
from the slaps and the punches that
the world pierce.

My hands look as strong
as those of any man.
They are dark and bruised
from doing the best I can.

My shape grew out of nurture and
love.
It fed the babies and soothed my man.
It hugged, comforted, cared, and
caressed.
It's endowed with beauty and strength
to withstand.

What does it mean to be me?
What does it mean to be beautiful me?

The answer appears
> in my big brown eyes
> on my tan face
> in my strong hands
> and by the flowing curves of my
> beautiful, ever so beautiful shape.

we SISTERS

Speaking of beauty we sisters have that.
In fact, we have so much more than that
And like a sold out party we're sho' nuf' phat!

We are the epitome of "ALL"
We connect like long distance phone calls,
Yet we're as different as an array of shops at the local mall.

Among we sisters there is a certain bond
Some say we're as close as a manicured lawn
or as tight as a haircut fresh from the salon.

When we know we sisters are near
We have no reason to worry and nothing to fear.
No wonder we're always there when we sisters need a listening ear.

We are a predetermined specimen, guaranteed to hold
For you know we sisters are sho' nuf' bold.
We're embellished in purple and adorned in gold!

See, as long as there have been sisters on this earth
we have populated the world, just by giving birth
For that gift alone man can't put a dollar on our worth.

And no man could ever walk our walk
'Cause we have more flavor than Lawry's seasoning salt.

And we sprinkle affection when we coo
as we talk.

We sisters are as mellow as a smooth
summer breeze
No wonder we have earned the never-
ending reign as queens
and have proven to have power to
make our men kings.

We should be celebrated from dusk till
dawn
Because we are like power forwards
and nuclear bombs;
One false move, and our kings become
our pawns!

Our mere existence proves a man a
man
Yes, we sisters are extremely feminine,
and adored like a love song played
again and again.

We are as soothing as herbal tea,
As tranquil as the beach and soft as the sea!
One touch from we sisters brings men to their knees.

To state our value is simply stating a fact
We sisters, well, we're all of that,
And like a sold out party we're sho' nuf' phat!

my BATH

My Bath

My Bath,
Oh, you just don't know
what it does for me.

It soothes
my aching muscles and
washes all my worries away.

It softens
my skin and moves and touches
me all over at the same time.

It hugs me.
It loves me.
It relaxes me.

It warms
my exhausted body and
sings to my weary soul.

It's full
of bubbles that transform me
back into the queen I really am.

My bath
treats me like a lady and reminds me
of all the nice things I deserve.

It hugs me.
It loves me.
It relaxes me.

My bath,
oh, you just don't know.

...Spiritual **Growth**

a prayer for my SISTERS

Dear Heavenly Father,

My prayer is not just for myself,
but for all my single sisters in the world.
My prayer is for hope;
hope for our current situation.
Lord,
I know that You're dealing with a lot,
especially considering it is the 90's.
But God, in case You haven't noticed,
there is a shortage of brothers.
You know what I mean, suitable black men, who are successfully building their lives.

See God, we sisters are definitely
prosperous and successful.
You have given us our piece of the pie,
for that we are truly grateful.
But now we have too much pie and
nobody to eat it with.

Don't get me wrong, Lord,
I know that You have put plenty of
brothers on this earth.
And some of my sisters have been
lucky enough to find their dream mate.
But for those of us who have yet to
receive such a blessing, we see it like
this:

A big bulk of our brothers took a few
wrong turns
and are no longer accessible to us.
Now let's see,
some are in prison or on drugs
and the others,
let's just say that they forgot we

existed after being accepted by our Caucasian counterparts.

I'm not particularly upset with those sisters,
because they finally figured out what we sisters already knew.
When You created a brother, I mean the kind who's spiritual, caring, intelligent, strong, and motivated, You broke the mold!
No other man is like a brother.
When a brother is together, he's really together.
Well, I think You know what I mean.

Dear Lord, what I'm asking is that You would bless me, and my other single sisters,
with the strength to withstand our period of tribulation,
until You bring our brothers, who have gone astray, back to us.

For Your word says that tribulation worketh patience and patience, experience and experience hope.
(Romans 5:3-4)

Currently, we are learning patience, gaining experience, and leaning towards hope;
hope that we too will one day meet a suitable man and finally be able to exhale.

Amen.

balancing ACT
As Told By A Typical Lady of the 90's

Balancing Act

Just when it seems the impossible can't be done
I go and surprise myself,
yet again.
Yeah, on the surface It may seem a breeze,
but to be honest
I, myself,
still shiver at the fact
that I manage to keep up my Balancing Act.

Sunday, Monday, and all the week through
With all of the things

I,
a mere woman, have to do

How do I manage to stay sane?

Well, I
say a prayer, take a deep breath and
just begin...

I
have a career that
requires all of my time
most of the time.
But when I'm not at work
I clean my home, clean my car,
and, of course, I clean
myself!

And in between...

I
find time to read interesting books,
Never refuse an opportunity to learn

something new,
That's why I plan just to catch a glance
of the 11:00 news.

I
volunteer at the Y, sing in the church
choir
and I belong to two social organiza-
tions.
(Isn't that the civil thing to do?)

Then I donate to me...

I
meditate
work-out to stay in shape,
eat healthy, think healthy.
attend church, plan for my future, hang
out with my friends,
and even though I don't have a man, I
keep myself looking good
for ME!

I
find time to have meaningful relation-
ships with my family,
both far and near
with whom I'm always willing to lend
an open ear.
I wake-up early, stay up late
So when slumber calls I don't hesitate...
to respond!

How do I manage to stay on top?"
Some may think "eventually she's
bound to flop!"

But I
disagree.
'Cause, from the start
it's has been an art!

It's innate
It's a blessed ability
that I

was graced with
by GOD!

It's called
WOMANHOOD,
which simply means
Having the nat
to become master at this balancing act!

dear DOUBT

You say I can't
But I can
You think I won't
But I will
You think you can contain me
I cannot be contained
You think you can destroy my dreams
My dreams are invincible

I am greater than you
I will succeed far beyond your limited boundaries
I have already climbed the mountain top and returned
I have built a wall that you can never devastate
I have claimed victory and IT is mine

I am Triumphant
I am Victorious
I am Jubilant
I am Dignified

I am a conqueror and I have conquered you!

a prayer for
WISDOM

Dear Heavenly Father,

Thank you for developing me into a beautiful and talented woman.
Thank you for being my protector and my guide.
And as I make my way along my journey
bless me with the wisdom to make intelligent choices;
The kind of choices that will prove beneficial for me and my family.

Bless me with the kind of insight that you gave to my mother
and her mother. For with your help, they turned out just fine.

Bless me to be a feminine woman; the kind of woman who is virtuous
and who takes responsibility for my own actions.

Bless me with the wisdom to embrace the right man for me;
one who will provide for me, protect me and give me the love I need.
And at the same time, Bless me to love and respect my man,
and to support him in every way I can.

Grant me the wisdom to know when to move forward
and the patience to be calm when I need to just be still.

Grant me the wisdom to accept those incidents which are out of my control,
And give me the strength to take action when it is necessary to take control.

Gracious God, God of Wisdom, thank you for answering my prayer.

I know that you'll always be there to give me more when the wisdom Granted by you takes me only so far.

Amen.

You can order Tajuana's *The Desires of A Woman, Poems Celebrating Womanhood* to share with your friends. To order, send your check or money order for 7.95 plus shipping to the address listed below.

The Desires of a Woman
POEMS CELEBRATING WOMANHOOD

_____ Consider having Tajuana Butler as a speaker for your next event. Check here and we'll send you a PR packet.*

Name _____

Address _____

City _____ State _____ Zip _____

Number of Books : _____ x $7.95   = $_____
Shipping: _____ x $2.00 per book = $_____
                            Total   = $_____

Please make check/money order payable to:
**Lavelle Publishing
2350 Spring Road, #30
Suite 250
Smyrna, GA 30080**

*Inquiries please call 1-800-862-9838

Lavelle Publishing

Please Allow 4 to 6 weeks for delivery

You can order Tajuana's *Sorority Sisters* to share with your friends. To order, send your check or money order for 17.00 plus shipping to the address listed below.

Sorority Sisters
A Novel

_____ Consider having Tajuana Butler as a speaker for your next event. Check here and we'll send you a PR packet.*

Name _____

Address _____

City _____ State _____ Zip _____

Number of Books : _____ x $17.00   = $_____.00
Shipping: _____ x $ 2.00 per book = $_____.00
                                Total = $_____.00

Please make check/money order payable to:
    Lavelle Publishing
    2350 Spring Road, #30
    Suite 250
    Smyrna, GA 30080

Lavelle Publishing

*Inquiries please call 1-800-862-9838

Please Allow 4 to 6 weeks for delivery